"Gunilla Norris brings a new awareness
of the sacred nature of all life."
—ANNE BANCROFT, author of *Weavers of Wisdom*

"Gunilla Norris' simple precepts for meditating
and living have a translucent quality.
We can all benefit greatly by observing them."
—THICH NHAT HANH

"I was almost breathless with wonder
at the beauty of Gunilla Norris' words—so simple
and yet so profound..."
—BISHOP DESMOND M. TUTU

"Gunilla Norris's remarkable reflections on friendship
inspire and guide us to the deep place where we can
'see the stars in one another.' A marvelous book to gift
the friends who sustain and enrich our lives."
—JOYCE RUPP, award-winning author

"Here, Norris brings her poetic prose and deep wisdom for
finding the holy within the human to a high view
of friendship where Spirit works within us to foster
the spacious, healing companionship of compassion that
connects us to all of life; within, between, and beyond."
—GREG JOHANSON, Ph.D. co-author of *Grace Unfolding:
Psychotherapy in the Spirit of the Tao-te ching*

"Along comes Gunilla Norris to reaffirm the possibility of
writing prayers about real life in today's world."
—RABBI HAROLD S. KUSHNER

MATCH

Bringing Heart and Will into Alignment
90 Days of Practice

MATCH

Bringing Heart and Will into Alignment
90 Days of Practice

Gunilla Norris

HOMEBOUND
PUBLICATIONS
Independent Publisher of Contemplative Titles
STONINGTON, CONNECTICUT

PUBLISHED BY HOMEBOUND PUBLICATIONS

For bulk ordering information or permissions write:
Homebound Publications, PO Box 1442
Pawcatuck, Connecticut 06379 United States of America
Visit us at: www.homeboundpublications.com

FIRST EDITION
ISBN: 978-1-938846-60-1

BOOK DESIGN

Front Cover Image: © ffolas (shutterstock.com)
Back Cover Image: Photobuay (shuttershock.com)
Cover and Interior Design: Leslie M. Browning
Interior Illustrations by Ashley Halsey | Visit www.ahalsey.com

Library of Congress Cataloging-in-Publication Data

Norris, Gunilla, 1939-
Match : bringing will and heart into alignment / by Gunilla Norris. —First edition.
    pages cm
ISBN 978-1-938846-22-9 (hardcover)
1. Spirituality. 2. Spiritual life. 3. Meditations. I. Title.
BL624.N673 2014
204--dc23

                                   2014005873

10 9 8 7 6 5 4 3 2 1

Each year Homebound Publications donates 1% of our annual income to an ecological or humanitarian charity. To learn more about this year's charity visit www.homeboundpublications.com.

Even a tiny ember can become a living flame.

_____

Contents

Introduction   xv
How the Practice Came to Be   xix

Part One: About Practice

I. Why Practice?   1
   Aligning
   Why Practice?
   Keys to Practice
   To Practice Requires a Practice
   The Bare Bones

II. Creating the Hearth   7
   Embers
   Gathering the Kindling
   The Heart's Flame
   Choosing the Wood
   Creating the Hearth

III. Learning to Be One Hearted   17
   Refining our Thinking
   Being versus Wanting
   Tending a Fire is Different from Burning
   Divine Discontent
   Getting Nowhere

IV. On the Way   25
Dedication
The Unexpected
Starting Again and Again
Nurturing Routine
Keeping the Matches

V. In the Desert   33
Losing Focus
Doubts
Expectations
Boredom
Correcting the Course

VI. Banking the Fire   41
Embracing our Journey
Burning Clean
The Warming Fire
The Illuminating Fire
The Concentrated Fire

VII. Sharing the Fire   49
Working with a Friend
Blessing One Another
When We Fail
Witnessing Change
Match After Match

VIII. Collecting the Embers   57
To Be a Loving Mirror
Friends of Fire
The Value of Support

Setting an Example
Rejoicing

Part Two: Practice

IX Living the Fire   69
The First Bundle
The Second Bundle
The Third Bundle

Closing   169

Introduction

For many of us there comes a time when we experience a nameless yearning. We feel that there is more to life than we are living. We sense there is a meaningful and timeless reality within, behind and beyond our day-to-day experiences. Sometimes we try to give this reality a name—God, Spirit, Love, Life, Presence, Intelligence, Reality, Being. We know that ultimately it cannot be named or defined. It is too vast. But it can be experienced.

Though we mostly ignore it in the stress and press of life, the yearning may persist, and we come to realize that we want to have a conscious connection to that vastness in which our lives take place and by which we are mysteriously supported. We also want to manifest our contribution to that vastness, to live more authentically. It is then we begin a search for a way to learn to be more focused, to live more of our truth and to bring our will and heart into union.

There are many traditions that offer ways to grow as persons. We want our spirit and our way of life to be all of a piece. To choose a path can be difficult. The method described in this book will not suit everyone, but it may be a start, a spark and a catalyst. It is concrete and therefore doable.

We have met people whose lives seem to be lit from within. We can feel how they have somehow faithfully attended to the particulars of their unique calling and are drawing strength and insight from an unseen center. We can sense that their will and their hearts are in alignment. It is towards such embodiment that our own journey urges us. This book seeks to provide a concrete method to learn to live our heart's desire, to contribute to the whole, and to grow.

Ninety days is a serious commitment that often leads to further and deeper practice. Though this book is about a particular practice it is my hope to bring awareness to what is needed in any practice.

The book is in two parts. The first part begins with a question: *Why Practice?* In this section thoughts are shared about the benefits of committing to a deep intention. The bare bones of this particular method are also described. *In Creating the Hearth,* personal and emotional reasons for practice are discussed as well as possible inner preparations for practice. *In Learning to Be One Hearted* ideas are given about how to better unify one's self. *On The Way* looks at aspects that a practitioner might find helpful on the journey. *Tending the Fire* focuses on what is needed to sustain a practice. *Banking the Fire* discusses the fortitude needed for a continuous commitment to practice. *Sharing the Fire* is concerned with the benefits of working with others. Collecting the Embers is about the gained joy and wisdom of practice. The second part of the book, *Living the Fire,* is composed of reflections for the ninety days of practice.

Many people have used this method and found it of help. My sincere hopes are that this will be true for you, and that you may journey to your heart's home where love is both the end and the beginning.

How the Practice Came to Be

For many years I had the illusion that if I understood something with my mind, I had it mostly conquered. I was a spiritual seeker. I studied. I grappled. I questioned. I wanted my interior life and my exterior life to be congruent. I apprenticed with wonderful people. I was in therapy for years. I read books. With right thought I truly believed I could control myself and perhaps my environment. I could *make* a difference, and I wanted to. No further work was needed if only I could study, understand and finally know; that is, think my way through.

Then my life fell apart. After 28 years my first marriage dissolved. We tried mightily to hold it together, but in the end we could not. Our grown children were in their own lives. After all was said and done, I found myself alone with my thoughts, and they were of no help at all. It was the beginning of conscious suffering and hence the start of earnest spiritual practice. Not thinking!

In my twenties and thirties I began to meditate, took yoga classes, learned t'ai ch'i and other mindfulness practices. I attended church regularly. I believed in the tremendous power of Love that is at the heart of the universe. In my thoughts I called that love, *God*. None of the above protected me from suffering. I found myself scared and alone. I was financially challenged, and I was grieving everything that had been precious to me. The void was inside and also outside of the black, curtain-less windows of my home—windows that I couldn't afford to cover—and that was true for my inner windows as well. Outside those windows were thick stands of leafless trees. Here, perhaps was the first real congruence of inside and outside.

To begin spiritual practice when you are deep in the woods is classical. Somehow I knew I was one of many in very similar circumstances. But being a statistic doesn't help. It's the day-to-day living that matters. And so I began with hesitant steps to try to find something I could do to help myself. I knew it had to be a spiritual practice—one I could maintain—one I could live with.

At first I put little red stickers on my mirror, on the dashboard of the car, on the kitchen counter. I chose red to remind me to stop, to take deep breaths and to try to believe that love was present exactly where I was. I stopped, I breathed and I didn't feel that love was present. I felt fear and grief instead. Soon I stopped seeing the red stickers. They fell off the dashboard and the mirror. The practice didn't reach my heart. I was willing to think something to be true for me when it was not. I hung comforting words from clothespins in the doorways. They were also meant to slow my anxiety down, to give me hope and a little encouragement. Before long I was ducking under the messages. I grew even a little irritated whenever I banged into them by accident in the dark. I knew I had to find something small and consistent that I would be willing to practice, that I could stick to. The issue was willingness, not thinking nor understanding. I had will but no willingness. Something inside me had to soften and open for that to happen.

After living with these failed attempts of one kind or another there was an enormous snowstorm one day. My old farmhouse was at the end of the line. I lost power for many days. At first I couldn't get out the door, the snow was too deep. I managed by cooking on a gas stove.

I scooped snow from the windowsills to melt for water. I made a decision then that I would have to have a wood-stove as I was sure this kind of storm was going to happen again. Four days in the deep freeze was not acceptable! As quickly as I could manage it, a wood stove was installed in the living room. Every day during the winter I lit it. One day, as I struck the match to light the fire I realized that here was something I was doing every day. It brought me light. It brought me warmth. All my senses were involved. I was doing something very practical which I needed to do for my daily life. I began to wonder whether I could make a spiritual practice out of this simple act? I have now practiced striking a match and mindfully watching it burn for more than twenty-five years. I no longer have a fireplace, but I have the inner fire. I want to share this practice with you. Here is a process that I have come to understand to be about working with deep inner longing, with willingness instead of will power, with daily, mindful presence, with creative expression and with surrender to that within that aligns us to our meaning and our purpose. I have not stopped striking matches. I do not think the learning process ever ends.

I will be continuing to learn new things and trusted old things over and over again in different ways. It will take the rest of my life. One match at a time it is doable. Each of us can become faithful keepers of his or her inner fire by tending to the flame. When we do, we illuminate our own lives and in the process we warm one another.

Part One

About Practice

I

Why Practice?

*Even when we forget
our deepest longings
are still awake in the dark.*

ALIGNING

We are all burning. Look at our digestive process. We burn food in order to live. We burn oxygen in order to breathe. Our physical bodies are furnaces for life. How could our wills, hearts and souls not be furnaces also?

We burn through the days and weeks of our lives. Any lit candle will burn out as will any fire in the grate. Before life is over could we realize that we are an ongoing fire? Then we might rightly wonder, what is burning to live inside us? What is our life truly about?

Of course we can exist without knowing anything about what we live for. Many people do, and however we might live our days, they will pass much sooner than we think. There is something smoky and acrid about just existing. The word exist is made up of ex and *sistere*—to stand outside oneself. How differently it feels when we live with and in our heart's desire, when we use our selves and our days for a chosen purpose. Then we do not mind that we are burning.

We experience being alive. We feel the passion and the joy of it. We find ourselves stoking that fire. And curiously we will find that we give ourselves easily to it. In time the effort becomes so congruent that it becomes effortless effort.

To align with the deep desire of our essence is always a joy. Then, though our days pass, we live within a different and much larger dimension. We are already bodies of light. We know biologically that our cells carry a kind of light. When we live from our essence we illuminate far more than we know. We can somehow sense that we are star-like. We are made of the very stuff of the universe. There is no greater belonging.

WHY PRACTICE?

It is so easy to think that understanding something is all that is necessary for doing or redoing anything. "I get that," we say with relief. But when it comes to our behavior, we do not change so easily. We continue to do what we do not want to do, and we do not do what we want to do. We are often startled by this, and sometimes shamed and shattered. The mind is so very fickle and needs training. The heart, on the other hand, is a steadier center for it is the primary home of willingness.

Living from our inner depths requires practice—daily, on-going practice. The effort itself weaves us into constancy. We become the weaver and the woven. And not for a moment can we have a smug sense of mastery. Exactly as in weaving, we discover the fabric of life as it reveals itself on the loom—an inch at a time. We cannot live ahead of ourselves. We must daily, consciously send the shuttle through the woof and weft of our daily events for the fabric of our life to be revealed. It is then we may come to know the cloth we are made of.

Mastery of life is the opposite of control. It is instead a willing participation with and a loyalty to those people, values, and concerns that are central to our hearts. It is ultimately surrender to Spirit that is at the core of our being.

Why practice? A good answer given by Parahamsa Yogananda is this one: "To work with God's happiness ever bubbling in the soul is to carry a portable paradise within you wherever you go."

KEYS TO PRACTICE

When we are too ambitious about what we are "to do" about personal growth or spiritual development, we set up an inner rebellion. It's a bit like going on a diet that is too enthusiastic or severe and then inevitably resistance arises. It seems to happen all by itself. For a practice to be of real use it has to make sense and be do-able on many levels.

- It needs to be simple and appealing.
- It needs to engage more than the analytical mind.
- It needs to be understood not as some kind of facile activity to solve our conflicts and woes, but as a means to be faithful to our journey.
- It needs to be sustainable.
- It needs to remind us of, and bring us closer to, the deep longing within.

By its continuous use, our dedicated way will bring us into territory that is ultimately not about effort, the use of the boot-strap-will, but about surrender to what we essentially already are. Practice will not make us perfect. It will make us faithful, loving and present.

TO PRACTICE REQUIRES A PRACTICE

Spiritual practice is a deep, inward formation disposed toward that of transcendent meaning to us. But we need some concrete nuts and bolts to do it—touchable things and visible actions to help us move toward that inward goal.

A painter to paint must decide whether to create on wood, canvas or paper using oils, crayons, encaustics or acrylics. The media the artist has chosen to use will, of course, shape the piece of art. But the life and meaning of the painting is not locked into those particulars. It goes beyond them. A cook will use a recipe to make something—a stew, an omelet, or a chocolate cake. Doing all three at the same time would create something unpalatable. We must chose. We must limit ourselves to something particular in order to be able to do it.

Human beings have used many things and many actions to structure their spiritual practices: circumambulation, bowing, chanting, conscious breathing, yoga postures, sacred reading, praying with beads and amulets and so on. All of them are means to get beyond means to meaning.

This practice uses matches and a matchbox to help us get out of whatever internal box we might be in. A match has a specific, practical use. Later in this book we will consider how a match can be far more than a piece of wood one scratches on a box to produce a flame. But for now it is a means to an end. We need something to hold on to while we explore what we want to give ourselves to and how to proceed. To have something small and utterly doable is steadying and very comforting.

THE BARE BONES

To begin this practice you will need a two and one half inch by four and one half inch box of kitchen matches. They are readily available in most hardware stores. You will decorate the box with images that are meaningful to you. More will be said about this in the next chapter.

Remove all the matches. Make a bundle of twenty-one matches. It usually takes about three weeks to begin a new habit. You will light the matches from this bundle first.

Make another bundle of nineteen matches. This is the second batch of matches you will light. You now have a total of forty matches. In forty consecutive days you will have begun to establish something. It will not always be clear what that is, but we know that in forty days in a desert one has begun to know the place a little better. It is a classical number for stripping down to essentials.

Lastly, make a bundle of fifty matches. That will make a total of ninety matches. By the time you have lit every one of these matches something will have started to happen inside you. It usually takes three months at least for a real change to take place. Perhaps that is why AA groups talk about ninety days of sobriety. We, of course, are not talking about abstinence from alcohol but about practice, self-possession, and steadiness—the stuff of presence and awareness.

For ninety *consecutive* days you will light a match with a purpose, a feeling or a desire in mind. If you miss a day, you must being again at the beginning for it is in the steadiness of ninety consecutive days of practice that a deeper level in you will begin to be engaged.

The burnt matches should be kept in a container of some kind.

Now you have the bare bones. The depth of this practice lies in your heart and your mind. For that you must seek what already burns within and longs to be lived and known. To represent this in images on your box will take some careful thought and feeling.

II

Creating the Hearth

---

*When it is enough
to be a hearth for Love's fire
we are free.*

EMBERS

Some people smolder along in life. Their love-fire is blocked. They are too busy, too distracted, too confused or too unaware to know that something alive and precious within is asking for airtime and attention. We all go through phases when we are not alive or aware of our inner longing.

Usually something painful has to happen to wake us up. We have to be choked off enough to pay attention, to experience real longing again. It is then we can catch the glimmer—that small, glowing light that signals we are more than we allow.

That glimmer is really an eternal ember of the soul. It knows of our unlived life. It is hot, and given even a little air and fuel it will go from ember to flame. We can trust this even when discouragement lays its wet blanket on our days.

One way to enliven our embers is to wonder. Wonder stirs up the ashes and brings things to the surface. We can ask questions of our selves that are not to be answered straight off but are to be lived.

They are meant to be open-ended invitations. These questions can be something like the following:

- *When was the last time I was engaged enough to for-get myself?*
- *What fervent promise to myself have I not kept?*
- *What do I not dare to explore that still tugs at me?*
- *What is Spirit whispering in my heart?*

Embers are left after a fire has burned down. Embers from our old fires remind us of what it was like to leap and dance with joy and passion. They are like focal points of longing

—places where future fires lie ready. But passion must be renewed again and again even if it is a passion for the very same thing we have always loved.

A way to keep our embers from going out is to question and wonder, for questions carry answers on their backs. Simply posing the right question can be a way to blow on the coals.

GATHERING THE KINDLING

Along with questions that are like good pokers stirring the ashes, we also need kindling to build a viable fire. Kindling, we know, is little stuff that ignites easily. We need enough of it so that strong flames emerge. That way the larger pieces, our deep passions that are going to burn for a long time, can catch on fire. We could think of kindling as little encounters we have that touch us. They may be lines in a poem or a song. They could be images in a book or a magazine. They could be poignant stories we see on the television or at the movies. They could be melodies, colors, smells or particular sensations that evoke some kind of recognition in us.

The word *kin* in kindling is a hint. There are things we are *kin* to that mysteriously belong to us through some kind of impulse-logic or familiarity that cannot be explained. We know them mostly through attraction. They are not fundamental desires, but they point to something more central. Spending time noticing what is *kin* to us is a way to begin to gather the energy needed to build a lasting fire.

If we would take some substantial time to notice what draws us we would gain much. Usually we just have little brush fires, things that attract us for a short while and are simply passing desires. The flame flares up and dies out. But if we were to be earnest in noticing what comes back to tap us on the shoulder or to whisper in our ears, we could in time gain some insight about what is really asking to be lived.

It is not hard to keep a file for pictures, poem fragments or journal entries. This is actually fun to do and most people are able to find things that inspire them because they have decided to be open and are willing to notice. It is almost as if what we are looking for is looking for us. Time spent this way is very fruitful. Whether we acknowledge it or not, the inner fire lies waiting. It wants to burn. It wants us to live what is central and true for us.

THE HEART'S FLAME

After collecting our kindling we might notice that there is a theme—a certain something that is being expressed by our choices. We might sense a longing for a quality of being— kindness, harmony, beauty, love, order, or mindfulness. We might notice a preoccupation with an issue of some kind—justice, the environment, education, healing. We might notice a yearning for a focus—a vocation, a home, a family, or a way to create or invent.

We might need someone with us who will listen to us as we explain to ourselves what lies underneath the words and the images that we have chosen. There is a heart's flame there, and it is alive and warmer than we know. The words and images that draw us are not casual and as random as we might think. They are hints from our deep self, from our intuition, creativity, and subtle wisdom as it connects with the Self of the cosmos. The hints that we receive from this center of our being are not practical and won't earn our living for us. They will not solve our problems. They will not bring us lovers. Yet in knowing more what calls us we can begin to make a furnace of our hearts. It also follows that in living out these images many life issues are answered and practical things are created as well.

The soul, the heart and the mind often have different agendas. We could perhaps say that the longings of the soul are like hard wood. They burn slowly and for a long time. Perhaps we even come into life with them. The yearnings of the mind tend to fluctuate more unless they are aligned with the soul and the heart. These unaligned yearnings are more like soft wood. They catch fire easily and burn up quickly. The heart brings our feelings to our yearnings and ignites our imagination. Without that engagement of our hearts we could not fully live our truth for we cannot go where we cannot imagine.

Perhaps we could say that our soul longings will last a lifetime—to be of service, to love, to praise, to trust, to make beauty. Our mind's longings are more practical—to get a job, to raise a family, to be healthy, to be well thought of. They are generally ego needs, which are important and part of being a whole human being. When our feelings, our imagination and our willingness—those heart capacities—align with our ego needs and our soul truth, we have the makings of a very good fire.

CHOOSING THE WOOD

As we get clearer about what our soul longs for we must seek the ego's consent and the heart's willingness. This consent and willingness is best represented symbolically until we can truly live what it means. We could say that these images and words are wood for our inner fire. Choosing them will take time, and the process is a kind of prayer. We want our lives to have integrity and to be returned to Life itself, for it is then that we experience fulfillment.

Aristotle said that the soul is not able to think without images. Consciously choosing an image to hone to is very powerful since we actually live unconscious images all the time. These are often unexamined scripts that color our lives. For example, we might have a subtle sense that we must work hard to be worthy, or that we are never enough. Perhaps we feel owed a lot, or that we are only worthwhile if we are givers. We can have a sense that we are more special than other people, or we can feel discouraged from the beginning and believe we will never amount to much.

We might think that images are only visual. That is not true. They can be things we have heard and incorporated. They can be body sensations, a felt sense of something being true for us. Very often these images lie in the background of our experience and operate within us as corrosive, smoking fires. We could call them negative imagination. They can lead us into conflict, addiction, loneliness and other forms of experience that separate us from ourselves and from love. Instead of allowing fear for our persons or our circumstances to silently steal our lives from us, we can consciously choose an image that carries meaning for our soul.

It is best to make both the words and the images simple and direct. A positive declaration of intent is the wood we are building our fire with. For example—*to be open, to trust, to forgive, to be grateful, to dare something, to love, to serve.* These are states of being. The images should represent these qualities to us easily and directly. We need to understand that they are declarations not only of what is possible but also what is beginning to be true and already at work within us.

CREATING THE HEARTH

After selecting an image or images and the affirmative words with which to represent our heart's longing, we can construct a symbolic furnace for our inner fire. All of us know we cannot live everything, but we can choose to give a strong focus to that something that is central to us. In so doing we narrow the field and increase the heat with our concentration and willingness. This kind of awareness acts a bit like a magnifying glass. Focusing sunlight through a magnifying glass on a specific substance usually creates enough intense heat for the material to catch fire. In a similar way we are focusing our hearts and minds in this practice to a burning center.

We are creating a symbolic furnace out of a box of kitchen matches. We glue our chosen symbols to the box. These will be ones we feel will help us remember to align our hearts, minds and spirits. The images can be simple or elaborate according to our taste. Often, though not always, in a standard box of kitchen matches there is a strip of cardboard that holds the matches together. It looks like a small bridge. We can decorate that strip and write our affirmations on it, or directly on the box itself.

It is not important that the box be a work of art. It is simply meant to be serviceable just as a fireplace is serviceable. We have mantle pieces to spruce up our living rooms, but when it comes to the actual firebox we want a no-nonsense place that holds wood and flames. This is often a relieving attitude to have when we make our symbolic hearths. They are not for show. They are for use.

We are now ready to make three bundles of matches as mentioned before. With string or rubber bands make a bundle of twenty-one matches, a bundle of nineteen matches and a bundle of fifty matches. With this done it is time to begin.

III

Learning to Be
One Hearted

---

*No matter how hot the fire
our true natures will not perish in it.*

REFINING OUR THINKING

There may be a temptation to think of this process as a kind of quick fix. Just do this weird thing and after ninety days all will be as you imagined. Voila! Would we say that about prayer and faith? We know better. It is simple common sense that any process to which we bring our entire selves with hope, love and passion will infuse us with the doing of it. The process is one in which by means of faithful practice an inward formation takes place.

It will not hold suffering at bay. Life has suffering in it, and we are always in one way or another participating in life.

No one will pat us on the back for doing it unless we do the patting. Soon patting will feel irrelevant to us.

We are not doing this process as a means of self-improvement, nor are we doing this process as a means of acquiring material gain or self-importance. There may, however, be acquisitions and personal gains that come out of the process. But they are bi-products and secondary gains.

We are doing this fiery thing to align our selves with our core, to discover and foster our true nature; the one imbued with and imbedded in Spirit. The heart's longing is to give full expression to who we essentially are.

We know an acorn is full of oak potential. It will go through many transformations that have to do with its evolution into more and more oak. In the end it will have branched out—full and rich in maturity and loaded with acorns. It will then naturally nurture life around it.

Implanted in our soul is the longing to become who we truly are. There will be things "along the way" that are important to us, but they are essentially "along the way" and will, by necessity, be left behind in time. Many illusions will be surrendered. The seed must shed its shell to grow.

So, too, we will have to shed what is in the way of true development. Perhaps that is the magic after all.

BEING VERSUS WANTING

It is good to examine what the actual motivation is behind our spiritual practice. When we experience a great discrepancy between where we believe we are and where we want to be, there is often an impulse to compensate.

We may want to be right.
We may want to be safe.
We may want to be acknowledged in public ways.
We may want control.

The key word here is want—and that, at its root meaning, is *lack*. If we engage in spiritual practice to compensate for lack we will not be practicing our connection to Spirit but a connection to lack, to being wanting.

Why not practice the joy of being instead of wanting? This requires of us a willingness to embrace and to understand that in the sheer fact of being alive we are already in a sacred contract for our fulfillment. In fact, as we acknowledge the truth of having been gifted with life and possibility, we are in a kind of prayer. We practice what we are open and alive to instead of what we think we lack.

Daily, as we strike our match and attentively pause, can we feel and underscore that there is already a correspondence between the longing of our soul and the possibility of its fulfillment? Can we know that in Spirit this connection is already established? This is not practicing wanting but practicing bringing our awareness to the rich potential already inside us and so to the possibility of bringing it to maturity.

TENDING A FIRE IS DIFFERENT FROM BURNING

Just as fire consumes a stack of wood and transforms it into heat and light—into energy—we must let go of many extraneous things to become our essence selves. One of these things is attachment to our practice even as we engage in it. There is a famous story from the Desert Fathers. It happened that Abba Lot went to visit his friend and mentor, Abba Joseph. We might assume that Abba Lot was having some doubts about his practice. He told Abba Joseph about his assiduous, meticulous practice and how hard he was working at it. Abba Joseph must have sensed the discontent in his friend, and how burdened he was with the work of it all. Abba Joseph didn't pat his friend on the shoulder or give him advice. He simply asked a burning question, *Why not become fire?*

The small, matchbox furnace we have made for spiritual practice is a reminding and signifying object, but it is not the stuff of the practice. Our passion and willing self-donation are the practice itself.

Because that is so, we will in time need to give up the ways our egos want to cling to all that is not central to our fulfillment.

We will have to give up the worry that we are not doing things right or well enough.

We will have to give up that we deserve something or are owed something because we are practicing.

We will have to give up insisting on specific outcomes.

We will have to give up those sneaky and relentless efforts at self-improvement—habits of thinking either too well or too ill of ourselves, and doing things to prove that we have rights and privileges that others do not have.

In the end what we find by practicing will only be found by practice. Anything extra we conjure up to add to the process only chokes the fire and will smoke up our work.

DIVINE DISCONTENT

How curious it is that within even our happiest moments there is yet an ongoing yearning, a kind of divine discontent. Perhaps it is because we are each a holy incompleteness even as we are also in some way already complete. We are most alive when we consciously practice alignment with our true nature. We do this in many ways but they are a moment at a time, a day at a time—weeks, months and years at a time.

It is good to remember that what we seek is also seeking us. At the lighting of each match we can be aware that a convergence is happening. Our conscious longing is attending to the deeper longing imbedded in our souls and ever at work. It is the longing to belong to Being, to awareness, to love and compassion, to creativity and beauty, to service, and to reverence for Life itself.

This divine longing is a fiery thing that returns again and again even when we have neglected and forgotten it. Given even the slightest fuel and air it will burn.

We are desired by Life itself to be fully alive. *Desire* from the Latin is given as *desiderare—to await from the stars.* Isn't divine desire an instinct to be more and more inclusive in Being and in awareness? When we practice heart-alignment we grow and release rather than possess and diminish. Our true nature will not be something to point to like a static object or a polished possession of the ego. It will instead be a blaze. As we recognize the heavenly light beyond our being we bring it more and more to being in ourselves.

Understanding this, we can let go of ever coming to an end of practice. We will never be finished. Life will seek life the way fire seeks fuel. We will always be the fuel and also the fire that burns.

GETTING NOWHERE

Moods are as fickle as the weather. Cloud-like they move in and out of our personal sky. Who knows what lack of sleep or too much food does to the body and hence to our emotions? Who knows what even minor frustrations in daily living kick off in our emotional make-up? It is important to realize that ultimately we cannot control ourselves. We try, of course, because we have to fit into society. Control is helpful by giving us guidelines, but it never gives us life. Trying to be in control we miss the depth that our hearts can experience.

We know severe self-judgment doesn't help. It often leads to acting out in the future. Self-improvement, though it feels good at the time, will make way for something else before long. We cannot base our spiritual life on such fleeting things. We must find something more substantial.

Becoming one hearted happens in surrender rather than in control. We must give up trying to create ourselves. We must release having to know before we can know. We must stop trying to be perfect whether in our own eyes or the eyes of those we admire.

It is safe to say we can only grow in our spiritual life by turning to the universal Love that continuously holds us in its embrace. Even when we do not feel it, we can turn our faces and our lives towards it. It means showing up where we are. Then *nowhere* becomes *now here*. We can always have *now here*—the only place where Love can meet us, where it can challenge us, integrate us, complete us and make us one with Itself.

Over and over we are invited to this feast. Day by day we can learn to wake up to the present and allow Love to have its way with us. In a certain sense it is a one step program. One-heartedness is really full participation in how things are and finding that Spirit meets us there. It is the central work of spiritual practice, and one that leads us into the world to participate more fully, becoming one heart with the heart of Hearts.

IV

On the Way

*When the will becomes
the servant of the soul,
the fire is lit.*

DEDICATION

When the furnace has been made and the match bundles assembled, it is time to begin the inward adventure. We have determined a direction—a true North, so to speak. Now the journey starts. Where it will take us is not ultimately up to us.

At the time of beginning it is good to dedicate the practice to something larger than our selves and our intentions. We can do this for particular people or circumstances, and for all others who long for their heart's home. We can take this journey of the heart into a larger sense of belonging—into the intrinsic task we all have of being more and more true to ourselves and more and more human. This will naturally make us present and concerned for one another.

A conscious act of dedication can be like a bulwark for us. As we do this with others in mind, we will somehow feel their presence for us as well. We are more continuously connected to each other and the world than any of us realize.

Dedicating our practice will help break down those habits of separation in us that are so rampant in our culture. When any one of us breaks through to live more fully from the heart, we open a way for others.

We know a healthy cell in a body supports the cells around it—so, too, we support the whole with our dedication and our practice. To speak this dedication out loud before lighting our first match brings a solemnity to the act. It is like an invocation, blessing the ninety days ahead. It is a declaration of intent and of willingness.

THE UNEXPECTED

Even as we have chosen our images and words and have our intention clearly in mind and heart, unexpected things will happen in the course of practice. It is almost as if in declaring our direction all that belongs to it begins to show up. Often these are the obstacles we must overcome to be in alignment with our hearts. These situations arise as if Spirit were asking, *Are you really serious about your journey? Here is a test of your willingness.*

It is important to embrace these unexpected encounters that arise because we have begun to practice. They are wonderful opportunities, though not always the ones we want. We actually need to practice against something challenging. It is like an athlete hitting a ball against a wall. The ball comes back, and we are required to pay close attention in order to connect with it again. Our ability to stay with practice will grow and so will our resolve.

Sometimes the encounters are immediate opportunities that align with our intention. Doors simply open. It seems a miracle. But more usually there are significant downs to the initial ups. Let's remember that we are deciders first of all. Then comes the work of acting on our decisions. Even in a deeply discerned willingness there may be a reservation or an ambivalence that we were not aware of. This wobbly place is usually not in our conscious mind, but it will be teased out in the fire of each day. More and more as we live out our willingness consciously, our journey will gather depth and strength. It will feel vibrant and real because we have realized our way, have learned by going where and how we need to go.

One thing we can count on is that the unexpected will feel luminous to us when one day we look back on our experiences. The first twenty-one days are our baby steps. In taking them we are learning to not let the focus go for even one day. We are learning to show up in obedience to our own depth and yearning. We are learning to be open to what in turn shows up in response to our intention.

Starting Again and Again

It may be that a day comes in these initial three weeks when we forget to light the day's match. Someone comes to visit and our usual routine is broken. We catch a cold. We travel or have unexpected deadlines. We can understand and explain why we forgot, but the fact remains that we forgot.

A strong temptation is to tell ourselves it doesn't matter. We'll just start where we left off. This kind of thinking is even more tempting when we have remembered to light eighty-three matches and forgot match number eighty-four.

It is in acknowledging that we forgot, and in beginning again that something is forged inside us. We are not going to lie to our selves or excuse ourselves. We are simply beginning again with match number one. This is not failure. It is truth and truth is universally known to set us free. In being truthful with a seemingly small thing we can trust ourselves a little more, and that trust can grow into larger and larger arenas.

Even if we have to start again many, many times, nothing is lost if we do not let ourselves be discouraged. We are learning. We are, in fact, training ourselves in consistency. We are in some senses more trust-worthy when we tell the truth about our forgetting than if we did the practice perfectly. Doing something perfectly is not as whole as doing it completely—that is, inclusive of mistakes and forgetting. This is actually true of anything we are lovingly engaged with.

In a way this practice is about starting again and again. It is striking a single, new match every day. It will be that particular match and no other. It will be that particular day of our lives and no other. We can only truly practice in the now we are in.

Nurturing Routine

Many people find that establishing a routine for their practice helps them not only to remember, but also helps them to settle into the experience in a deeper way.

It is good to pick a consistent time when we will be with the practice.

This can be any time, yet many say the start or the end of the day works best for them.

It is good to be in the same location when we strike our match. The familiarity of such a place is centering and reassuring.

It is good to create a little sanctuary for our matchbox so that it, too, has its own place in our home. It is after all a special, signifying object we have created.

When we do these three things we allow an associative process to build within us. We know from experience that certain places and times of day, certain odors and temperatures have particular meaning for us. We can almost immediately touch a past experience and its physical and emotional effect on us by re-experiencing sensations like these: the warmth in our grandmother's kitchen—the evening sunlight on the porch—the smell of cut grass—the softness of a particular blanket—birdsong in the morning light—the feel of rain on our cheeks and so on.

If we are consistent about where and when we practice, our unconscious selves will be brought closer to our conscious selves. Over time the scratching sound of the match as it is lit, the smell of sulphur, the glow of the flame, the heat near our fingers, the familiarity of doing this simple act again and again will bring our chosen focus more deeply into our being.

Keeping the Matches

When we strike a match and blow it out we are apt to toss the little, charred stump in the trash. But it is helpful to keep the burnt matches. Here are some reasons for this:

When we are uncertain whether we have struck our match for the day or have lost count in some way, we have the burnt matches as a record.

A spent match is a very graphic symbol of a day that has been lived.

Accumulated, the matches make it plain that our lives are really so many countable days. Each one is precious and they will eventually come to an end.

As we see the matches pile up, their very presence may somehow ask us if we are actually living our heart's deep longing.

Also in sheer accumulation, they are verification and confirmation of our practice and that we have been faithful to it.

Honored and kept in a bowl for the duration of the ninety days, the matches will remind us to honor our selves and our intentions. At the end of the practice time we might create some small ritual of conclusion with them. Just as we began with a ritual of dedication, we might end with a ritual of acknowledgment. If we have practiced with friends, the remains of all the burnt matches might become kindling for a fire of celebration.

We are a rushed society—a culture that continually looks for new, splashy things to have or to consume next. Small, ordinary things make little impression on us. We tend not to stop to digest our daily round—the sweet, un-dramatic events of living. We forget to savor. This often happens in spiritual practice as well. We do not take the time to digest what we have, what has been learned and gained in the doing. Keeping the used matches is one simple act to counter this tendency. By acknowledging the used matches as having worth, we too become worthy.

V

In the Desert

Stripped,
the heart begins to open
to what is real.

LOSING FOCUS

One of the hardest things about spiritual practice is keeping the focus and keeping it fresh. Once the verdant, excitement of deciding on and starting our practice wanes, we find that what promises to be a greening for us, a garden of possibility, is also a desert.

Practice can be so wonderful at the start, and it can become so arid after a time. It seems to be the same old, same old, day after day, and we can feel it to be dry and relentless as if we were exposed to too much sun-light. We just want to close our eyes and shut down, find shade and go to sleep. We are in a barren place.

This feeling comes to each of us in different ways for we are actually brought by our initial willingness into those places where we are inwardly unwilling. This is hard to face. We will find our desert and it won't be in bloom.

Here it is a matter of attention. How we feel needs to fade into the background a little. We don't have to love our practice, nor feel hopeful or devoted. We must just do it with open eyes and with attention. Real observation is asked of us. It is to notice, with respect the act of scratching the match-head on the strike plate of the matchbox, of seeing the fire flare up. It is to not skip one moment of the flame moving along the wood of the match. It is to feel our fingers grow warm as the heat comes closer. It is to be awake as our intent brands us into full owner-ship of it in mind and in body. Even blowing out the flame is not to be missed, nor the confirmation inherent in placing the used match in its bowl for keeping.

Attending, attending, objective attending. Not wavering. Our desert will bloom when its time has come, when it is the season for blossoming.

DOUBTS

It is disconcerting that in making a strong decision to practice, and in applying the decision to do it; we can yet come up with a sense of doubt about the whole thing. A little voice inside might say, *what good is this really? How very silly, maybe downright stupid to light a match a day! What's really being accomplished with this? And it is time consuming and messy to boot. Ninety days of this—is this crazy or what?*

These voices are rarely loud, but they are a crowd and often sneak in one by one with reasonable sounding tones of voice. They eat away at our stance about practice the way the sand at the beach falls away under our feet with each new wave. A little doubt, repeated over and over can bury us. We sink in our resolve.

How can we defend against erosion? First, it is good to be aware that once we make a commitment we will usually be tested. This will be true whether it is about this practice or any other matter.

Secondly, the doubting thoughts we hear should not be argued with for there will be another reasonable counter argument for every one we have. It is better to inwardly agree saying something like, *you are probably right. You have a good point there, and I'm still going to do this thing that sounds so stupid and silly.* We are not disputing anything. We are just proceeding. The word *and* is the little bridge back to another day of faithfulness.

Lastly, we will discover something about our doubting, some under-current. It might be a fear of looking silly to our selves, or a fear of failing or a desire not to waste our time. Under these doubts there are always fears—fears that show up as doubts about any choices we might make. How freeing to find out that it is not the end of the world to look silly to our selves or to fail. We learn much more in failing than in achieving. As for wasting time, we do it every day in so many other ways.

Over time we will have a greater ease and freedom in teasing out the subtle ways our minds can work against our hearts. To become one-hearted we must face both our big and our little doubts.

EXPECTATIONS

A big difficulty in our spiritual development is having expectations. It is confusing and paradoxical to set an intention, to mobilize our spirits in its direction, to feel a yearning for that intention and to nevertheless let go of the outcome.

The way Spirit works in our lives is so mysterious and ultimately so wise that we must surrender our expectations of when and how things should happen. We are not to skip having a clear intention about what we want to give ourselves to. That is the heart's deep work. But, deeper still, is an open and continuous willingness to embrace whatever outcome our yearnings set in motion. That will most likely not look like what we expected.

Some of us may have heard of the young girl who prayed for something she wanted very much. Her prayer request ended with, *I would really like this if it's good for me and for others or something even better.* We often miss the something even better because we are locked into our insistence on a particular result. It is true that desire is needed to get things going.

We could think of it as Spirit's longing for more life within each of us—a longing to grow, to live, to give and to express. It is a joy that seeks us as much as we seek it. When we allow joy its way, it goes where it can, entering the nooks and crannies of our lives, illuminating us until fruition is made visible. But when we force anything we stop what is a natural progression. Expectations by their very nature force things—they silently push and insist and create resistances of all kinds.

As we light each match we know we cannot do the burning for it. We must allow it to burn as it can. Sometimes the flame peters out almost immediately. Sometimes it is bright and steady to the very end. Striking a match every day is meant to reaffirm our intention to align with our heart's deep joy. We "match" our wills with our willingness. Slowly expectations begin to fade. We will want what is— the vibrancy and reality of experience, the knowledge that we are faithfully *on course* and that the fruits of practice will appear at the appropriate time.

BOREDOM

Most of us live at a pace that is faster than is good for us. Used to such a tempo we seek to be entertained and to be pumped up even in our down times. Our movies are full of special effects to thrill or shock us. Our television programs are peppered with violence and advertisements. We are not given to settling down, and so we do not tolerate humdrum very well. This, of course, enters our spiritual life. We want special effects there, too. We abhor to be bored.

But what is boredom? It is a demand of sorts isn't it? *Do for me! Engage me! Interest me! Bring me something new!* Some people will do dangerous and sometimes crazy things to create engagement, to have their thrills so as not to experience feeling dull.

Having a rich spiritual life is not something that can be done for us. It is by its very nature something we must give our selves to. That is why some people do not stay the course. Without plenty of continuous and visible excitement, they are bored.

Any time we are bored we can be sure that we are somehow not attending. We are not present and are asking someone or something to do the showing up for us. We are actually passing the buck. So to be fully present for the less than thirty seconds between the time we strike the match and the time we blow it out, trains us subtly to be more present in the rest of our day. We are needed every second during this little act. Without real attendance we could burn ourselves or light the house on fire.

If we could extend this kind of attention to more and more in our lives, we would find that we can slow down, that we feel less stressed, more awake, and not in the least bit bored. We would be in deep attendance, instead, aware that our lives are blazing.

Correcting The Course

After forty days of striking a daily match we begin to sense more fully what our original intention was about. Perhaps we were seeking to be less judgmental. Perhaps we were asking for more engagement in a creative project. Perhaps we intended to be more careful of our bodies or our resources. Perhaps we were opening ourselves to more intimacy. Whatever it was we had in mind to embrace with our hearts and our spirits is now sure to be clearer to us. We have had a chance to experience our willingness and our resistance at a deeper level.

Having more experience under our belts may entail that we change the words of our affirmations to be more precise. Or it may be that we must alter the way our matchbox furnace looks in some way to better represent our new insights. We may place a small, significant object in our box as a further reminder to stay on course.

It is often in desert experiences where we are tested that more clarity emerges. Many people experience that obstacles appear out of the blue that have something to do with their intention. They seem to be tests about our resolve. It is almost as if all that is in the way must appear for us to work with it in order to be able to receive our intention. If this happens we should actually be encouraged. People tend to throw in the towel at this point. But if we take any obstacle as a sign that we are more fully on the way, then, what is in the way will be seen as an integral part of our journey. We will know it as an opportunity for greater authenticity.

When obstacles appear we are more likely to be discouraged and forget to strike our daily match. This may happen quite a bit in the beginning. If we remember how many times we fell off a bicycle before we learned to ride one, we will take this in stride. We will just try again.

Forty days is a very short time. If in restarting we spend two months or three or more we are yet on course. We are not lost or a lost cause. We are in willingness training. We are in joy training, aligning with our heart's willingness and our spirit's wisdom. That is worth all the time it takes.

VI

Banking the Fire

What is progress but our love fully lived?

Embracing our Journey

For a fire to last a long time it must be banked. This is a matter of placing the wood in such a way that it will not burn too quickly. It also means that the flue in the fireplace needs to be partially closed. What is valued here is the slow, intense heat of coals—not great flames that will soon burn out. With a banked fire one can cook or keep a home warm through the night. With a banked passion we can sustain a long journey.

To persist in practice for ninety consecutive days we must learn to bank our fire. We need to cultivate and embrace certain attitudes and insights for a prolonged period of internal cooking. It is a paradoxical wedding of our passion and a realistic conservation of energy. It is a deeper entry into willingness.

When we can embrace limitation we grow to be more dependable for ourselves and for each other. We need to understand we are not embracing limitation for limitation's sake. We are embracing it for a larger purpose. We are choosing what is sustainable over what is thrilling or dramatic. It is easy to understand that this can be applied to many other matters than spiritual practice. Clarifying what we have chosen to be about is the first step to making it possible. We can see the framework that we must work within, and that is ultimately comforting.

We need limits to feel where we are. Working *with* them we grow *beyond* them. Central to this acceptance is to remember that we have chosen our intent. It is we who have selected it—no one else. We are therefore beginning to accept responsibility for what is meaningful within us and for aligning with it.

The deep acceptance of a self-prescribed practice will not tolerate excuses, blaming others, forgetting or any other manner of avoidance. If we want to grow in spiritual maturity we cannot say, *I didn't mean my own commitment.* For ninety days we must simply and slowly cook, allowing our intention to simmer inside us and to bring us into greater wholeness. We need to re-choose our journey each day. We need to feel and want the fire of it.

BURNING CLEAN

One attribute to encourage in ourselves is patience. Patience is like an enduring coal that keeps being vital by holding heat a long time.

Impatience, on the other hand, is a kind of smoldering. It spews acrid smoke on our longings and intentions. It's a bit like putting the accelerator to the floor when both the hand brake and the foot brake are engaged. Impatience wastes us.

Impatient, we lack the ability to live the in-between. We don't delight in the journey itself. We hold the destination as the be all and end all. Any of us who have traveled know that arriving is only a small part of traveling. It helps to know that being on the way is the way. Free of impatience we can appreciate the discoveries and subtleties that belong to our chosen path. Instead of only arriving somewhere specific, we have the opportunity to become our journey.

So much is overlooked or dismissed as unimportant when we are impatient. Consumed by impatience, we are not teachable. The strange, the new, the old understood from a different perspective, the comforting, and the discomforting cannot become part of us. Impatient, we only have insistence. In the end it is impoverishing. We do not give ourselves time to grow.

Patience, however, honors and humors the in-between. Of all the virtues it is the one that serves as a connecting bridge. It allows us time to verify, to go back to what we already know, and to move forward to the unknown. Released from demanding particular outcomes, we have time for backing and filling until an inner consolidation takes place, and we move forward with greater confidence.

Impatience creates anxiety. It demands that something be true and secure before it can be. Patience, on the other hand fosters trust in the moment's beauty and nourishment as well as the moment's challenge and truth. Impatience smolders. Patience burns long and clean.

THE WARMING FIRE

We can never be warmed and comforted by our practice if we hurry our inner growth. Our souls will not be forced. A deep and truthful resistance is guaranteed to arise when we do so. If we understand impatience as being driven by expectation, then we might see that hurry is largely driven by fear. As human beings we have so many fears—that we essentially are not enough, that we won't be safe, that we are the ones who must handle it all, that we will be shamed, judged or otherwise diminished if we aren't productive and keeping up.

Our culture asks us to multitask, to do things fast, to be efficient and to acquire more and more and to get ever more things done. Our souls ask us to be. Over time we gain a sense that practice is not something *to get through*, but something *to live*. It is a matter of duration, and we'll need many more days than ninety days of practice to learn this. We'll need a lifetime to learn and relearn the same thing at a deeper and deeper level.

We can practice, perhaps, by allowing more time before and after striking our match of the day. We can ask that all the parts of ourselves be present as the match is lit. We can allow the heat and warmth of the flame to be more than a physical reality. In these moments we can stop our hurry habit and let the ancient sensation of gathering around a fire be a reality for us. Around a fire the soul knows itself as flame, as light with light, as a particular meaning within a greater meaning. It is a sensation of presence and of belonging.

Match by match we learn to exchange hurry for inner harmony.

We live both in time and in timelessness. When we let go of hurry we can feel both. The present moment grows large and boundless, and we sense how it is imbedded in forever.

The Illuminating Fire

If we persist in staying conscious our practice will reveal who we are. We will find our usual excuses, our tendencies both to *overdo* and to *forget to do*. We will discover the expectations we have of our selves, of others and of the practice. Stripped of illusion we will see ourselves as in a well-lit mirror, and we will have a chance to know that we do not have to be better than we are. We simply *are*.

For the ego this is a real burn. It is scorching to give up the insistence that one has a special status that is better than others or worse than others—victimized and therefore excused—or privileged and therefore entitled. The list is endless and is always about being a special case of some sort.

To accept our selves as is, is to accept that under all our moods and self-judgments, under all the vicissitudes of our thinking about ourselves, lies a fundamental innocence which does not need improvement. It needs simply to be allowed to be. It is this innocent being that is able to bear the flames of love. Like the salamander depicted in ancient alchemy, it can live in fire. Our egos cannot.

If day after day we relinquish our self-explanations, self-excuses, and self-improvements and allow our hearts to have their true affinities instead, we will become light for others. We will be fully present, aware and able to enter awareness itself—that place the ego avoids for there it must relinquish being *someone separate*. Ego demands are mostly compensatory or addictive, even if they show up in small and subtle ways,

Our heart's affinities, on the other hand, are there, given to our souls as if from always. We do not need to be improved to feel them. We need to move slowly, daily towards them, burning away the demands and deceits the ego sets before us. It is in this way that we experience the difference between happiness and joy. The ego wants happiness—its daily dose of satisfactions—not a bad thing in itself except that it is generally a substitute for real joy. Our souls want the real thing—full participation in being—with openness, innocence, and vulnerability.

THE CONCENTRATED FIRE

When we have a long way to go it is essential to put one foot in front of the other steadily and, in a sense, light heartedly. That means just doing the practice without worrying much about how we are doing.

Having a specific intention to hold in mind and to travel with, we can let go of tantalizing detours. We can picture this as if we were traveling in the dark with a flashlight. Our intention casts a light and illumines just enough ground to take the next step and the one after that into the un-known. The whole journey can be made in this way. Each step becomes significant and particular because we are able to feel it, give it its due, and because we do not go ahead of ourselves or live beside ourselves.

This kind of focus is a relief. With a chosen intention we select more easily what belongs and what can be forgotten. There is less confusion. We see just enough of our way to continue. Yet it also makes our progress stronger.

Strong and light are qualities that make endurance possible. We find as we cultivate them that we can do more. Day by day embracing our intention, it begins to embrace us. What we long for comes to meet us. This is mysterious, yet many people have experienced it. As they commit to their heart's deep yearning, and act on behalf of it, things begin to happen to aid the process. The opportunities, the people, the necessary links show up in strange and lovely ways.

A new task is then added to our practice—the task of receiving—allowing our selves to be helped. We can allow the burden to be carried by Spirit as much as it is by us. Over time we will come to experience that we are strongly partnered. Committed to the heart's deep intention to the real and truthful expression from our core, we will be given extravagant help.

VII

Sharing the Fire

---

*With friends we travel further
and better than alone.*

Working with a Friend

When we practice with another, the practice grows warmer just as an extra log on the fire generates more flames. To practice side by side for ninety days, committing not to miss a single match we intensify our inner work in tandem. Many experience that being witnessed and companioned they are strengthened, and that their commitment grows.

How tender and vital it is to have someone who knows of our heart's longing and who supports us in aligning with it. We are then known *heart to heart*. We offer one another not only sanctuary but inspiration and courage.

A very sweet way to begin is to share what draws us, and what it is we want to develop in ourselves. Stating this out loud, and hearing our own words in the presence of a friend is very powerful. Also making the matchbox furnace together opens us to greater intimacy as well. We are now not only in something internal and private, but also in something external and visible. Though the matchbox is mostly symbolic it allows a way for inner and outer to meet and be witnessed.

To strike the first match together is a ritual of deep intention. If one of us forgets, we know it will be both of us who have to begin again. Not only does it matter to us individually that we are faithful, it matters to us as a team as well. We will not want to fail one another.

Though we will most likely be striking our matches at different times and in separate places, we can agree to meet to talk and to share after twenty-one matches or after forty. We can arrange what best suits both of us. In this mutual agreement we are parts of a whole. It will soon be apparent that whatever we realize in practice will somehow belong to both of us. The struggles and insights accrue to each of us though our intentions are unique. We will soon feel them as aspects of a larger work—the growing of our souls. We will become more and more transparent to one another, seeing more and more deeply that we can only give what we have in our hearts. When we do, we paradoxically attract what we are giving away.

BLESSING ONE ANOTHER

Every day we have an opportunity to bless our practice partner. This extends our practice and theirs as well. Anything we fully do with heart and soul reaches far beyond our small, individual lives.

Having been inspired to practice is not a private matter. We are imbedded in Spirit. We are individual expressions of Spirit; therefore we embrace the whole by being true to the inner work we are called to do. Understanding this in a deep way, we will not be so tempted to compare ourselves with our friends or long for their inner work. We will want what is ours, and we will know that by being who we are, embracing the union of our heart and our willingness, we are blessed and are able to bless others in turn.

Here, too, any preoccupations with outcomes of practice begin to be irrelevant. Belonging to Spirit, as we already do, is what matters. We are part and parcel of it, too limited to understand the vast order that is at work, yet growing to know that we can trust it more and more.

Possessiveness—what belongs to whom—is not relevant either. As it is, everything belongs to Spirit. Comparison—who is better than someone else—is useless. We are all holy and precious. And if we are jealous, it is only an indication that we have not yet been willing to receive the sacred gift of who we are.

The only question to answer is—are we practicing faithfully? When we do, the blessing grows. We return the gift to the Giver. As it says in the Koran: *Allah asketh naught of any soul save that which He hath given it.*

We tend to suffer because we lack awareness or because our small egos take over. It is by no means simple to let go of our separating patterns. It is hard work. Yet, spiritual practice lets us discover that much of our suffering is useless and self-made. Spirit is always for our essence and our inner growth. Blessing each other and practicing together we support this. One person's faithful practice holds space for many others. Two persons or more make a field of blessing.

When We Fail

When we make a commitment to practice together we are opening our selves to mutual support and to victory as well as to mutual suffering and to failure. Practicing together we will feel light and shadow as one—resistance and willingness as parts of one another. We are signing up for a willingness to be human with each other, which includes failure.

One of us will forget to light a match one day. If it is match number nine we will take it in better stride than if it is match number eighty-nine. We will be tempted *not to tell* each other of our mistake or to *vehemently tell* of our disappointment if our friend lets go of the practice for a day. If we are truthful with each other we will be open about our feelings and so have an opportunity to go beyond them.

We will have a chance to see that it is the common effort that brings us light and love, and so closer to our intent. We will in time not *want to get there* without our friend, wherever we imagine *there* to be. This feeling becomes even more intense when we practice as a group. We discover that *doing it right* is not as important as starting over and continuing *to do it*.

Whatever we are working with in ourselves and together has a depth and a range that is far beyond ninety days. What is set in motion by this practice is a profound dedication. When we fail and begin over, we are learning discipline and its deeper truth—devotion.

We learn more in failure than in success. We learn how attached we are to being right and faultless. Practicing through failure we come to know that we are loveable as we are, that we are worth the time. As the matches burn we realize that the light we are asking for is already inside, and that we can be that light more and more with each day. Starting again and again we claim our willingness to be light with Light. In this there is no failure.

Witnessing Change

A lovely aspect of working together in a partnership or in a group is that we can witness the changes that occur in our selves and in each other's lives. Sometimes our companions can notice these changes far better than we can ourselves.

There will be a stronger timbre in the voice, a lighter step, a more hopeful outlook, a glow to the skin, and a straighter back. These may be very subtle signs at first, yet they indicate that something fundamental is occurring not just in the mind but also in the body. We embody a new truth. Then when changes in our life circumstances begin to surface, we are not too surprised.

It is more who we are than what we do that is given to the world. When we give our selves fully to our inner and outer tasks we are aligned. We flow. Other people can feel it. Responses come. The opposite is also true. Haven't we noticed that when we are out of sorts, the toast falls in our lap jam side down? The car won't start. If we are secretly angry, we often find that someone speaks to us angrily for no good reason. We are in resistance and resistance comes back towards us. It boomerangs. When we are in our spiritual truth, however, living our soul's desire and so connected to Spirit, we find the world more in resonance with us. Giving our love away, our love returns in the form of opportunities, new relationships, better health and so on. Aligned with our core and its expression, we are in flow.

To witness one another grow and flower over time is a high privilege. Since love begets love, our witnessing under girds the process much like fertilizer given to a plant under girds its growth. It is important to celebrate and acknowledge one another. We do not fully have what we have until we consciously receive it. Our companions on the way are living mirrors. Through their witness we can better acknowledge how we have grown, and what we now can embody. To have, and to know that we have, is profound, for to them that fully receive more shall be given.

MATCH AFTER MATCH

Match after match is struck and a flame appears, flares brightly and burns. Day after day we can grow in awareness of our centering passion. We can foster it, and burn for the sake of it. We do not mind giving ourselves away to what matters because joy is there. We know we are fully alive. Irenaeus said *that the glory of God is the human being fully alive.* Having been given life are we not to live to the fullest?

As companions we can see that each of us is a living fire. We can also feel how we are co-creators of meaning. This tends to lift and encourage us further.

Let's remember that everyone is an expression of Life that has never been before and never will be again. It is also true that the whole of Life is present in any and every part within Life. We can never fall out of that reality or be separate from it. We represent it in individual ways. How poignant is this understanding—how necessary then to support what we can in one another. Together our lives become Life burning with the joy of sheer being, the joy of becoming, and the joy of participation. We are here to give away who we are to each other. This is the sacred task of willingness. We do it by aligning heart, soul, and body. We do it by expressing our deep desires in creative ways. We do it by working together.

As unique flames within the great fire of existence, let us burn for that which matters to us, sharing our warmth and our light. There is no greater privilege for a human being.

VIII

Collecting the Embers

*In appreciation we find
that excellence belongs
to everyone.*

To Be a Loving Mirror

When two people or a group of friends practice together the energy of their common effort supports each individual and also supports the entire group. A bonding occurs that is subtle and powerful. Though not in realms of sensible reality, we can nevertheless feel and see each other spiritually and so be strengthened. Our intentions are brought more into focus and into action by this common commitment to practice.

When friends practice together they could be thought of as being in a room of mirrors where every other person in the group reflects every person. How deep it is to know that to see ourselves we need to be seen. As we share the images and meanings we have given to our matchboxes, we can experience the reflection others give us. That not only furthers but also validates our efforts at aligning our hearts and wills. Our intentions become more substantial. We can feel that they are more alive and are gaining ground within us.

The accumulation of energy that happens when a group shares at this level can be felt and brings renewed commitment and often further insights into what we are individually trying to do. There are often common longings as well as shared themes, and this is not only heartening but soul befriending.

To mirror one another is sacred work. We need to keep our reflection process clean so that our friends can see in our eyes that we have understood what they are trying to do in their ninety day journey and that its meaning is deep for them and will bring a transformative change into their lives.

To align with our core and allow that to be witnessed is a fierce and bonding experience. As loving mirrors for each other we will be charged with sustained commitment, and we will be privileged to share in each other's blossoming.

FRIENDS OF FIRE

Each match has its very own moment. Working together we strike them one by one in our separate dwellings, at different times of the day, and for personal intentions that are often deeper than thought can take us. By now we understand that we are each learning not only to keep our inner fire lit but also to become that fire.

We must trust that our companions are "at work" not only for their own sakes but for ours. Any gain in consciousness, in soul-alignment and wholeness, is for the whole of existence as well as for the individual. When we trust this to be valid and true, our faithfulness in practice gains weight and stability. We are less likely to let ourselves down for we know that when we do, we let everyone else down as well. And in reverse, when we practice faithfully our gain is multiplied and is given to others. We are mutually profiting in ways that cannot be measured and yet are deeply true.

To remain faithful over time is what builds trust in our selves and in others. It cannot happen unless we are consistent. To trust each other spiritually is very serious and penetrating. When we are betrayed or let down in that area of our lives, the wounds go very deep and are often extremely hard to heal.

In a culture that is so addicted to speed and immediate gratification this long and patient process to build trust is not very popular. Yet the rewards are great. What seemed difficult at one time becomes much easier over time. We learn that we can sustain a focus, that we can be inwardly present, and that we will and can do what we said we would do. This is a deeply tempering process. Like good steel we will in time and with time cut through our habits of postponement, our excuses, our spiritual laziness and forgetfulness. Trusting ourselves and trusting each other we are much more able to cut through to that true place where we are unalloyed, where we align with our essence and live from it.

THE VALUE OF SUPPORT

A tree does not grow without a strong root system, a deep and grounded support. We, too, if we are to grow into our full spiritual stature need grounding and support.

Support can be experienced from within. Perhaps we sense that we are supported by the vast Love that created us and sustains us. We are drawn to align with it and to express it in our lives in the unique and individual ways we are called to do. Without the inward experience we would most likely not take up a spiritual practice such as this one.

Support must also be experienced from without, however. Like plants that are able to bear much fruit, we need to be staked. We need the presence of others to hold us steady and rooted to the task. This is not a crutch—it is a necessity! When we see a woman with child we tend naturally to support her. It is instinctive to serve the bearers of new life. When we practice with friends, be they men or women, support can be understood to be this mutual awareness that we are pregnant with life.

Just to be seen as potent is sustaining. We are humbled by the recognition that what is in us matters, and that others lovingly perceive us as able to bring it into being. Then, when support comes in more concrete ways—helpful suggestions, information, insights, time and presence—we can feel that we are staked by the help of others. In fact, we have a mutual stake in each other.

We cannot go where we cannot imagine. Sometimes the imagining of another person for us is the very support that let's us see what we are capable of. When we imagine for and with each other, a kind of magic happens—our mutual beauty and potential takes root and begins to grow.

SETTING AN EXAMPLE

We may not be aware that every moment we are setting an example. Such self-awareness could bring us to our knees. Yet it is true that we humans tend to copy one another both for ill and for good. We influence all the time, and often without knowing that we are doing so.

Practicing with others we cannot help but see each other's struggles and triumphs. Every victory won is inspiring. And the valiant struggles that do not end in victory are nonetheless examples of courage. We are always learning from each other.

There are great heroes and heroines of the spirit we can emulate. As a group or as a pair of friends we can share the same books by people who inspire us. Perhaps we will also recognize in each other meaningful habits of thought, speech and action that we want to emulate. The most inspiring example that we can set for each other is to be faithful to our practice...to keep our promise to ourselves.

We will not ever really know how we influence or impact one another. That we do is a fact. If we just stay simple and persistent in our efforts something of value cannot help but transpire though it is not up to us what that will ultimately be. We do not have that kind of control or prescience. But a deep intent, lovingly and constantly held in heart and mind will, in time, bear fruit, and will become visible. In this we can actually relax. For with concern turned to practice and not to outcome or evaluation, we have gained the freedom to experience, to be and to discover. We can forget proving and demonstrating and give ourselves instead to living fully for our heart's deep yearning. There is no better example to set.

REJOICING

In rejoicing we repeat a meaningful experience by recognizing it, relishing it, savoring it with others and returning to it many times. It is possible to rejoice alone, but it means so much more to us when we can rejoice with beloved others.

Whether we accomplish our intention or not, we have at every moment the occasion to rejoice. This is because practice itself becomes joy. We are a home for it, and we are at the same time at home in it. Practice with others is a shared joy...a field of opportunity that continually enlarges our spirits and our lives.

Intentions are directives to our minds. They focus us. As we practice we move from thought into more and more embodiment and being. Our intentions then tend to change. Whether our intentions are large or small, they are always catalysts for further embodiment. They lead us into the field of love and possibility where we are invited to give of ourselves and to manifest a life fully lived.

This may be dramatic for some and simple, though equally as precious, for others. It is the very same field— ecstatic, inclusive and ever changing. Inherently we are that ecstasy. We burn with that fire. As we recognize how our souls belong to that field of joy and how our hearts are drawn to consciously align with it, we cannot help but rejoice with every small step taken, every little realization digested. In the mystery that we are and the mystery we are becoming we hold one another in the fire's light.

It is perhaps in rejoicing that we come closest to matching ourselves to the joy inherently within us. This little practice is a daring and humbling gift we can give each other. With it we can honor the dancing light that flickers deep within our souls.

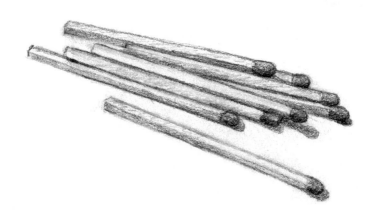

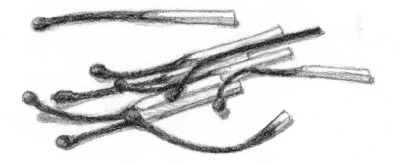

PART II

Practice

In order for a match to ignite
it must be struck.
So, too, in life we must be struck
by something truthful
to wake up.

IX

Living the Fire

Ninety Days of Practice

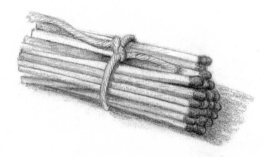

The First Bundle

Choosing to light a first match with intention and then the next one, and the next after that—what will happen—an inner bonfire or worse, nothing?

What will happen if we are really present every day for the few vibrant seconds when the match is burning?

There is such a difference between wondering and entering Wonder. That first step, that intentional act, followed by another step, and another can change everything.

Day I

Today is the beginning of practice.
The first match is burning.
Will we know we are burning, too,
and that *how* we live our lives matters?

Day II

The flame moves along the wood.
It follows what feeds its existence.
We do not need to hurry
our spiritual life, but we can follow
inch by inch the direction of our yearning.

Day III

Day by day, match after match
we are breathing in light.
We breathe in the warmth.
By inspiration we can grow
to know that we are also light.

Day IV

Without the full engagement of our hearts
how can we live our truth?
However long it may take us,
we can let these matches burn away
whatever blocks the way.

Day V

Practice is simply practice
and leads to additional practice.
There's no need for us to make it be more.

Day VI

Every match is like all the others,
yet it is particular.
There won't be another just like it.
It will burn in its own unique way.
This day, too, is particular.
We must live it in our own, unique way.

Day VII

By inward communion
and guided by Spirit we can sense
what is ours to do and what is not.
In a measured way we will not take on more
than is ours to accomplish.
But in what we do, let us be
as thorough as a flame consuming wood.

Day VIII

How good it is to love what we already love.
The changes we seek come from having love,
not from wanting it.

Day IX

Can we forget ourselves
for a little while? Can we just be simple
like this moment of burning—
concentrated like a flame?

Day X

Awakened to our soul's longing
we are marked.
It is a kind of branding.
Something inside us knows
what our hearts belong to.

Day XI

Striking the match of the day.
the flame blossoms up.
It is a wakeup call.
Please do not miss
a single precious thing!

Day XII

It isn't what we think
we should be able to see and understand,
but what we do see and understand that matters.
When we look with love it all matters.

Day XIII

For less than this minute
—the length of time the match burns—
could we turn ourselves over?
Could we let go of control
and just be?

Day XIV

Answers reassure us
but it's the questions that keep us
knocking on the door.

Day XV

Each day we say our intentions out loud,
These are the words of our longing.
We wrote them down
at the beginning of practice.
Now we string them one by one
on the shining thread of affirmation.

Day XVI

To do this one simple thing
—not as a habit nor as an obligation—
but to do it for its own sake
is a great and curious freedom.

Day XVII

How hopeful are beginnings.
At the start all seems possible.
Perhaps it is necessary for us
to just keep beginning.

Day XVIII

Can we learn that there is no thing
we can give to our selves or to others
that is a more valuable gift
than our pure and willing attention?

Day XIX

To be in the house of belonging
we must carry what we love
over the threshold
and be married to the tasks
of daily care.

Day XX

We strike a match. We smell smoke
and sense the fire deep within.
Instead of smoldering
can we make room for love,
and give air to the flame?

Day XXI

The first bundle is finished.
The spent matches lie in a bowl—
symbols of days lived and gone by.
They are mostly ashes,
but we can remember
to keep kissing what is now.

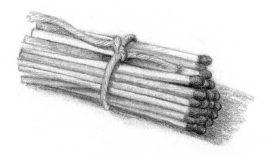

The Second Bundle

We spend hours performing the needful,
yet the soul can live on thirty seconds
of fiery encounter and be filled.

Day XXII

Practice is being in a landscape—
lush greenery, deep rivers, deserts, swamps,
cataracts and craggy mountains.
Each match illuminates where we are
—a part of everything.

Day XXIII

Inside we hear voices:
Things should have changed by now!
Isn't a spiritual practice supposed to
make me feel better, not worse?
Expectation is such a desert.
It makes me brittle and dry as a bone.

Day XXIV

So far there doesn't seem to be
any results from our efforts.
Why should we bother to go on?
What makes a journey worth the while?
When we falter like this, doubts swarm and buzz
around us like mosquitoes in a swamp.

Day XXV

Forgetting to practice is easy now.
We seem to do everything but
what we promised we would do.
If we do not love and care
for our inner lives
we will make orphans of our hearts.

Day XXVI

Here's another match, another chance,
a moment of light.
We may think it's insignificant—
too small to matter.
But we know it is moment by moment
that life becomes momentous?

Day XXVII

Some days we sit in the shadow
of our unlived joy.
It's a craggy peak,
a mountain we can't climb,
but we can make camp,
strike a match and light a small fire.
We can warm ourselves.

Day XXVIII

Wanting something other than what is,
we seem to stumble into cacti and stones.
Not wanting at all, or wanting too much,
we create wastelands where
we become strangers that do not see
the given as gift.

Day XXIX

There are efforts that are so meaningful
that we don't mind how difficult they are.
And there are others that feel like useless work.
How much time making ourselves look good
to our selves or to others are we going to waste?
We'll just have to do it again and again—
a sure way to burn out.

Day XXX

An old root of the word
to *suffer* is to *allow*.
We won't skip suffering as long as we're alive.
Then why not suffer the right thing:
allowing our heartfelt longings
and acting on their behalf.

Day XXXI

Can we be lit again and again—
drunk with experience
and lavishly present
to just how things are?

Day XXXII

The flame creeps closer to our fingers.
We feel the heat. Intimacy is like that.
It wants to burn through our defenses
and yet leave us whole.

Day XXXIII

How many matches are there in a box?
How many days will be ours?
Match by match, aren't we learning
that the number of our days
is not as important as the number
of our *lived* days.

Day XXXIV

The genuine giving of ourselves
to any moment is a gift we give ourselves.
It is then the love-fire burns
and claims us for itself.

Day XXXV

One day we slog through the mud
of long held attitudes.
Another day we climb
the stony hill of assumptions.
Each burning match is so tiny.
The inner task is so big.

Day XXXVI

It may seem to us now
that all the things in the way
of our intentions are showing up.
These are the angels we must wrestle
until we get a blessing from them.

Day XXXVII

Instead of holding fast,
holding back or holding in,
could we behold how,
even in darkness and difficulty,
love is still present?

Day XXXVIII

We need to own whatever of anger,
disappointment and sorrow there is in us.
Coming clean, the daily flame burns
with a brighter light.

Day XXXIX

No one escapes who he or she is.
Inside we have heaven and hell
and that unrelenting yearning
to become all that we can be—
homes for love and possibility.

Day XL

By choosing to light this match
and then the next one,
and the next one after that—
what is happening to us?
Nothing?
Everything?
Neither?
Both?

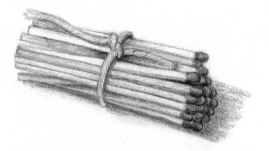

The Third Bundle

The chambers of our hearts
hold more than we can ever know.

Day XLI

This third bundle is big and daunting.
We do not really know
where we are going.
Yet something leads the way—
a trust in going
by simply continuing to go.

Day XLII

How unrelenting is the gap
between what we long for
and what we fear cannot be.
It is a wound.
that will not close by force of will.
It heals only in willingness.

Day XLIII

This bundle seems all about endurance.
We hope that the carbon of doubt
will not gather and clog everything.
We ask for the inner wick to be trimmed,
to burn clean.
We ask for simple strength.

Day XLIV

The days of our lives pass away
one by one. They won't come back.
By the light of our matches we see
how precious is Monday,
how holy is Tuesday.

Day XLV

We brush my teeth. We comb our hair.
We clothe our bodies. We take daily care.
When we light each match
are we not given care
even as we take care?

Day XLVI

By now the images on our boxes
have changed a little in meaning.
They seem broader or deeper
and take us out of thought
into silence.
Could it be that what we long for
also longs for us?

Day XLVII

As the match burns we see
that it is the flame that is active
and the wood that is passive..
When we move from making things happen
to allowing Love to work us
we feel the heat of co-creation.

Day XLVIII

This yearning to be connected,
to be in awe and participation
is so full of ache and beauty,
of satiety, impermanence and loss
that is must be the mystery of joy.

Day XLIX

Moments of understanding pass.
Joy dissolves in a dishpan.
Our inner lights are dim again.
Yet something remains.
It is a growing trust
that we can somehow know
without knowing.

Day L

To forget a match this far into the practice
may feel very defeating.
But since every day is a first day
how much can it matter?
Beginning again we'll
just match along.

Day LI

We are members of a family,
members of interest groups,
of friendship circles and work teams.
We are always part of some larger body.
But when we light each match
we are re-member to our deep yearnings.

Day LII

Gazing more deeply each day,
at the flame as it burns,
and feeling it inside,
we know we cannot fail.
Outcome and practice
are somehow becoming
one and the same.

Day LIII

For no good reason a match is lit
and does not burn.
There's wood but no flame.
From time to time we live a gray day—
There are notes but no song.
There's no reason to reason.

Day LIV

Over time the meaning our boxes have for us
will change. The images are the same,
but our understanding of them is different.
Best not to try to figure things out
and to let change simply happen.

Day LV

Just as the acorn is a full grown oak
in potential, we already contain
what can be.
Match after match,
a light shines on the truth
of becoming.

Day LVI

After the match catches on fire
we plainly see
the meeting of fire and wood—
a precise convergence.
Attention to our lives is like that.
We are warmed.

Day LVII

The present is
always available—a gift
to unwrap, to savor
and to receive.

Day LVIII

Every match shines
further than we will know.
We are supported by the faithfulness
of countless others.
We sense how everything waits
upon everything else. There is no separation.
This match burns in and for
the wholeness that is.

Day LIX

The soul leaps and burns for its own joy.
Our work is not to be efficient
or functional, but to be alive.
and immersed in the unfolding
beauty of all that is.

Day LX

We are not alone except
when we make ourselves so.
We are not insignificant
unless we think it to be true.
When we live with fiery audacity
every scrap of unworthiness
is burned away.

Day LXI

It is possible to stop
the endless efforts at self-improvement
and turn towards self-acceptance instead.
It is possible to stop our constant hedging
and planning. It is possible to trust
that we each are necessary parts of the whole.

Day LXII

If we relinquish thoughts about our value—
how big or little we think we are—
we grant Love the last word
and enter silence where we come to know
that we are beyond worth.

Day LXIII

Daily we offer up the light
and the dark of what we are
and allow both to burn.
We are being refined by Love
in order to be love.

Day LXIV

To feel beloved
is to come to realize
that we are known
and entirely revealed
in our strength, our frailty,
our faults and preciousness—
nothing left out.

LXV

We are not self-made.
In the end we don't belong to ourselves.
We belong to Love's purpose.
Since everything has been given to us,
we have nothing but gratitude,
to call our own.

LXVI

Can the fire of Love
so penetrate every layer of resistance
that we can come to feel this tempering
not as suffering but as a gift?
Can we remember that we have
an entire lifetime for
our metal to be refined?

Day LXVII

On the surface
our habits and choices may seem ordinary,
but it is in the deep chambers of being
that we experience the difference
between a life lived in devotion
and a life constructed
according to the ego's restlessness.

Day LXVIII

When we live by the ego's command
our lives tend to be tense
and full of effort. We feel stress.
for we are separated from
the Love that holds me.
Aligned, we are free to spend ourselves
and so in the end we become ourselves.

Day LXIX

Living in and for
that of Spirit in us
is not selfish. It is self-full—
the only true gift we have to give.

Day LXX

There is a deep surrender
in the acceptance of being beloved.
It lets us tend to the real work
of holding light and being it.
There is no need to polish our egos.
Shining happens by itself.

Day LXXI

We have so many ways
to avoid being claimed.
But once our hearts are given
they are made tender.
Then we will know that a day lived
without tenderness is a day not lived.

Day LXXII

Not worrying about what we have,
or what kind of impression we make,
we relax into Spirit. This is freedom.
Something new burns in our cells—
a sense of hope and humor.
Something soft and quiet
surrounds our hearts.

Day LXXIII

Match by match we are learning
to align and to listen.
It takes more time than we ever imagined,
but we are not wasting time.
We are gaining it.

Day LXXIV

We have a dual citizenship.
We belong to tick tock time
and to infinity.
Love is the constant in both.
We can't understand this mystery
with our minds, but
our hearts light up with it.

Day LXXV

Daily we need reminding
until the one who is longing
and that which is longed for
are burning as one.

Day LXXVI

Faithful practice
is like any journey.
We may think we know where we are going,
but it is what we learn
along the way
that is the real destination.

Day LXXVII

When a goal is reached
we may not know it
because we have already moved beyond it.
We can trust
that Love knows no bounds.

Day LXXVIII

We won't find meaning
somewhere or elsewhere.
It will be found
exactly where we are.

Day LXXIX

We light an ordinary match
and imbue it with significance.
The light we see
and the light we are
burn together.

Day LXXX

We may forget.
We may neglect our practice,
but the heart's core is
like magma. It burns
and does not got out.

Day LXXXI

Fire always seeks to include more.
It cannot stop its mandate to burn.
Neither can love be stopped
in its mandate to love.

Day LXXXII

The song is in the singer,
the dancer in the dance.
The flame is in the burning.
We are in our practice.

Day LXXXIII

Whether we recognize it or not,
our deepest calling
is always calling us
in Love's name.

Day LXXXIV

The bowl of burnt matches overflows.
Here are the signs of days gone by.
Looking back we can see forward, too,
trusting the truth that no love
is ever wasted.

Day LXXXV

In quiet receptivity we find
living coals among ashes.
We are given new life
over and over again.

Day LXXXVI

In Old Middle English the word kindle
meant to bring forth children,
to give birth.
This is the task of the kindled heart.
With each match we are asked
to be fertile, to be mothers
and fathers of life.

Day LXXXVII

The matches lie silently in the box.
They do not need approval
or recognition.
They are simply available.
Could we be as un-selfed
and do the same?

Day LXXXVIII

Striking a little match each day
is both ludicrous and holy.
It is a tiny passionate act
and brings our deep longings
to Love's great furnace.
It is a prayer.

Day LXXXIX

We match ourselves to the moment
and new worlds come to be.
The heart is vast.
It holds the fiery paradox
that we are already whole
and yet constantly becoming.

Day XC

Ninety days have passed,
but our journey has not ended.
Deep within our hearts
love's fire always waits to be lived.
This is joy and it is free.
It costs everything.

Closing

Ninety days is a long time to hold a focus, and yet it is also just a beginning. We know that aligning our hearts and wills with Spirit and daring to live our longing is a process for a lifetime. It cannot be hurried. It will have its ups and its downs. There will be moments of lucid understanding and moments of dullness and discouragement. But not to be aware of and care for our inner being is merely to exist. It is not to live.

When we live from the heart, we make our daily decisions very differently. We doubt less and worry less. We listen frequently to the still small voice within us. We dare more, for we know that our task is to be faithful to the love placed in us and not necessarily to be successful in a worldly sense, though that may be a side effect. When we allow the flame of love to be our focus we let the chips fall where they might more easily. We realize that we have no control, and that responsibility for outcomes does not ultimately lie in our hands. So many things are constantly conspiring together beyond our ken. We can only tend to and love what is given us in the moment. But by so tending we can confidently drop our little match in the furnace that is Spirit's outpouring passion. We are all bits of heavenly fire. Practicing we learn to be timely in timelessness. We learn to rest in the heat of developments, leaning on the

Love that is always present despite our fears and coveted expectations. Over time we will come to know the Love that made us and will not let us go. We will experience that we are in it and of it and function as it. Then even our failures will be put to good use.

This practice, done alone or shared with others, can bring about unique and wonderful ways to release our deepest longings, allowing joy to burn brightly and reveal what we in essence are.

*In the end, where we are going
is where we already are—deep in the Heart
that holds everything.*

About the Author

Gunilla Norris' parents were world travelers in the Swedish diplomatic corps and so she grew up essentially in three places—Argentina, Sweden and the United States. As a child she was given a rich exposure to different languages and cultures.

She received her B.A. from Sarah Lawrence College and her M.S. from Bridgeport University in the field of human development. She is a mother and a grandmother. She has been a psychotherapist in private practice for more than thirty years and has felt privileged to accompany many people on their journeys to growth and healing. Her special love has been teaching meditation and leading contemplative workshops of many kinds.

As a writer Gunilla has published eleven children's books, one book of poetry and six books on spirituality including: *Being Home, Becoming Bread, Inviting Silence, A Mystic Garden, Simple Ways,* and the award-winning *Sheltered in the Heart.*

Reflecting on her success thus far she comments, "When I published Being Home in 1991 I did not know that I had begun a series of books on what I now call household spirituality, or the practice of spiritual awareness in the most mundane and simple of circumstances. Together these books seem to me to be like a crystal with many facets. They are part of one thing and yet shed light from different perspectives on the humblest of our day-to-day tasks. It has always been my understanding that when we are really present in our daily activities, our lives become more luminous, filled with love and grace."

www.gunillanorris.com

HOMEBOUND
PUBLICATIONS

At Homebound Publications we publish books written by soul-oriented individuals putting forth their works in an effort to restore depth, highlight truth, and improve the quality of living for their readers.

As an independent publisher we strive to ensure that "the mainstream is not the only stream." It is our intention to revive contemplative storytelling. Through our titles we aim to introduce new perspectives that will directly aid mankind in the trials we face at present as a global village.

At Homebound Publications we value authenticity and fresh ideas. From the submissions process where we choose our projects, through the editing phase, through the design and layout, and right to the crafting of each finished book, our focus is to produce a reading experience that will change the lives of our patrons.

So often in this age of commerce, entertainment supersedes growth; books of lesser integrity but higher marketability are chosen over those with much-needed truth but a smaller audience. We focus on the quality of the truth and insight present within a project before any other considerations.

WWW.HOMEBOUNDPUBLICATIONS.COM

"The great Catholic author Thomas Merton has said, 'a spiritual life is a disciplined life.' To open to our full spiritual possibilities requires dedicated practice. In *Match*, Gunilla Norris offers an exceptionally beautiful and surprising new form of practice. It has all of the best and most essential components of classical spiritual practice: it is appealingly simple, practical, honest and real. Ms. Norris creates for us a safe and sacred container of great beauty into which we can pour our longing for spiritual awakening. Contemplatives of all stripes will be grateful for this gift!"
— Stephen Cope, author of *The Great Work of Your Life*

"...Once again, Gunilla Norris has gifted us with her wisdom—this time with clear, engaging and inspired practices to rekindle our soul's longing and our heart's deepest desires. I'm in the business of lighting sparks, and this book goes to the very top of my recommended reading list!"
— Debbie Phillips, Founder, Women on Fire

"...Gunilla Norris has created a simple and profound 90 day journey that transforms this metaphor into both a spiritual path and a sacred art form. A spiritual path in that it will deepen and nourish your practice as a seeker of inner truth. An art form in that like alchemy, it will transform you into fire itself."
— David Gershon, author of *Social Change 2.0*, co-director of Empowerment Institute

"Gunilla Norris is an alchemist who transmutes ordinary daily actions of living into spiritual practices aligning heart and soul. ...*Match* is a tool that is unsurpassed in igniting the heart and soul of leadership to make a positive difference while tending the interior fire."
— Ellen Wingard, author, Mindfulness Based Leadership Consultant

"*Match* has my vote for best spiritual practice book of the year. Having had the pleasure of reading Gunilla Norris's trademark brand of household wisdom for years, I now know how she does it. *Match* reveals the deeply personal, profoundly creative, easy-to-do daily spiritual practice that has carried the author through decades of authentic living. ...*Match* offers an extraordinary opportunity to join in a spir[...] phenomenon that is bound to spread like wild fire."
— Kate Sheehan Roach, editor, *Contemplative Journal*

"...Self-improvement readers all too often receive books of admonitions that f[...] more on end results than the actual nuts and bolts of the process itself. *Match* [...] about firing up a course of action and committing to its enactment; and if 90 [...] of focused meditations and reflection sounds easy—it's not. ...This is only the be[...]ning of a lifelong journey. ...Those ready to undertake such a journey will fin[...] better starting point than *Match*."
— D. Donovan, *Midwest Book Review*

HOMEBOUND
PUBLICATIONS
Independent Publisher of Contemplative Titles
WWW.HOMEBOUNDPUBLICATIONS.COM

ISBN 978-1-938846-
9 781938 846601

US $16.95 SELF-HELP/SPIRITUAL

P8-DFZ-539